GATE

Ilze Kļaviņa Mueller

LAUREL
POETRY
COLLECTIVE

ACKNOWLEDGMENTS

"Picture from My Cousin" and "Invisibility Poem: Lesbian" were published in *Looking for Home: Women Writing about Exile*, ed. by Deborah Keenan and Roseann Lloyd (Milkweed Editions).

"Sea," "Presences," and "Long Enough" were published in *Water~Stone*.

"An Enormous Wish" was published in *A New Name for the Sun* (Laurel Poetry Collective).

"Closeted Lesbian Infiltrates Latvian Knitters' Group" was published in *Calyx: A Journal of Art and Literature by Women*.

"Laima, Goddess of Fate" was published in *100 Words*.

"My Mother Said" and "Child Little Body" were published in *Hedgebrook Journal*.

In this book, I have used excerpts from Paul Zweig's poem "Space Is the Wake of Time." The epigraph for "The Poem of My Life" comes from Adrienne Rich, "Twenty-One Love Poems," II, in *The Dream of a Common Language: Poems 1974-1977* (New York: W. W. Norton, 1978).

ISBN 0-9728934-2-3
Library of Congress Catalog Card Number applied for.

Printed in the United States of America.

Published by LAUREL POETRY COLLECTIVE,
1168 Laurel Avenue, St. Paul MN 55104
www.laurelpoetry.com

Book design by Sylvia Ruud

My thanks to my mother, who recited poetry to us, her three daughters, as far back as I can remember; my mentors Deborah and Roseann, whose joy, support, and encouragement have helped me write the poems in this book; and to my family, friends, and fellow poets—my loving community.

CONTENTS

GATE

GOLDEN PRIMROSES

In each life, the moment
when we first know
greed, anger, ignorance
when the angel with the sword
bars the way to the Garden
where on a spring hillside
under last fall's leaves
gleam golden primroses.

She our first Eve
knew too but pushed away
the knowledge wanting
to stay childlike forever
while the man at her side
raged against the world
and the furrows in his brow
etched themselves deeper.
Between these two we grew
as best we could
without words
to speak our dreadful knowledge
trying all the while
to forget.

No one told us
why primroses are called
the *keys of heaven*
or that the Garden of delight
is ours to enter still,
that the golden keys
were never lost.

CHOICE

Drive down the dirt road—well, really two faint tracks in thick grass. The dragging belly of the car brushes white and purple violets, huge soft dandelion blooms. There's the creek, a dare. Will you cross? The gravel bed looks solid, but suppose the wheels mire? Suppose there's no momentum and you have to step out in the quick current, walk in your soggy shoes back to the highway, wait for rescue? You make the decision, head into the glittering water. The car is steady as a ship, even speeds up on the other side as the wheels find purchase. Your companions let out a breath, laugh, and applaud your daring, but you are still thinking of that long hesitation.

———

LAKE

My ancestors believed that lakes roamed the sky in the shape of heavy rain clouds, waiting for someone to call them by name. If a lake heard its own true name, it would descend, covering the hapless person who had called out, his cows, sheep, fields, house and all. A lake is overhead now, waiting for its name to be called. Or can it be that someone's already done that? White water descends in streams, gushes through downspouts, covers sidewalks, roads, parking lots, no longer soaks into the saturated backyards, is planning a vast lake bottom where our cities still twinkle their lights. It won't be long now and Lake Agassiz will be back under its ancient name in its old site, mirroring an empty blue sky or the stars at night. Those who venture out in sailboats or ferries will see the tips of skyscrapers just below the surface, modern reefs, home to schools of agile silvery fish.

SEA

When I was very little, my mother says, I watched her wade into the sea on a Latvian beach and crawled after her with energy and determination, and who knows where I would have ended up if she hadn't noticed, plucked me from the shallows, borne me kicking to the big striped towel back there in the dunes. The waves still glittered beckoning to me and I uttered a mighty wail of disappointment: I was beginning to realize that there were obstacles between me and what I longed for. If she hadn't stopped me I might have learned to swim, floated to the opposite shore of the Baltic, been raised on Swedish ground, and grown up to look at customs officials with the confident eyes of nationals of neutral countries who have nothing to fear and no favors to ask.

PICTURE FROM MY COUSIN

I wanted to write about these children on the beach, but what can I write except that Baiba is seven and Kristine is nine and Ruta is two and Peteris is six and Agnese is five, and they're my only two first cousins' children, and they live in a little town in Latvia, the same one where I was born, and they're all in the picture together as they picnic on the beach, and they're fairhaired, and some of them look alike and others don't, and the little one has a big white floppy ribbon on the top of her head, and she pouts and won't look at the photographer, and Baiba the seven-year-old has her finger in her mouth and her shadowed face looks pensive, and Peteris grins at the camera, and Agnese scrunches up her face as she peers at the shiny lens and reaches for one of the strawberries in the big white enameled bowl, and she's wearing a little tee shirt and little round baubles at the ends of her thin little pigtails, and it's all so normal, the cups, the thermos, the spoons, the big bowl of berries, the children after their swim, the summer grass tall behind them, the shrubs thick and dappled with sunlight in the background, while I am filled with a pain and an anger beyond words, because it's the summer after Chernobyl, and what secret death will they eat with each sweet berry, what danger hides in each drop of salt water they spit out as they come up from the glittering waves shouting, "Look, Ma, I can swim!"? I want to shout, "Don't eat!" and it's too late, and what is the use, and my heart clenches with fear and with love for these children, the summer after Chernobyl.

MIGRANTS—1949

And then we saw the coast, low and green.
There were no tribesmen dancing around a fire.
A few white sea birds followed the ship.
What sort of life would we have
in the strange land? Already some of the passengers
had thrown their overcoats into the ocean.
Would it always be hot? The immigration
officials spoke of a country filled with sunshine
where the future was bright. An old woman
stood at the railing, wiping tears on her sleeve.
We felt reckless. Anything could happen now.
It was no surprise that on the billabongs
the swans were black, and huge flocks
of parakeets wheeled above our heads,
flashed blue and yellow like many small flags.

An Enormous Wish

To be stripped of everything,
Like the night on the island
In the middle of the wide Congo
As lightnings split the sky,
And no way to get back to the other side.

We fled the warm shallows,
Huddled in a shack around the fishermen's fire.
Somebody played a tape of "Hey, Jude."
I was no one, I had no past, no future.

When dawn painted the sky yellow and pink
And the motorboat came for us,
I wanted to stay in that place.
To be stripped of everything,
Shivering but clean.

Flames from a driftwood fire,
The small blackened fish they fed us
With great kindness, the strange words
Of that song—like signs in a language
For the deaf, elemental, but saying so much
About what matters.

I Come to America—1954

Looking backward all the way
like migrant birds, their flight
reversed completely by a hurricane

The Flowers of Evil in my lap
as I stare at the wake of the SS *Orion*

Through swarms of flying fish
past leaping dolphins
gold and scarlet clouds their backdrop

Ignorant of the future, without dreams

As full of prejudices as a country dog is full of ticks

$149 a month at Meridian Mutual, *One happy family*
says the CEO

Hostess Cupcakes—lunch, one dime,
kidneys and canned beans for supper
because they're cheap

Sunday, on a park bench, earnest and bland
the old man next to me explains
race hatred—Shem, Ham, Japhet

I get off a bus—*Honey, you in the wrong
neighborhood*—a kind brownfaced woman
points me back to where folks like me belong

Here, too, they have flags and marching bands
that make your feet want to move
to someone else's music

and paperbacks at the bus station
tales of torrid passion, violence, strange perversions
loneliness, despair

At night on the Greyhound bus in the middle of nowhere
seeing little houses, the porch light on
circled by moths

A few clothes, a radio, half a dozen books—
lighter than ever before

The arrogance of nineteen years: I know
all there is to know, and this isn't worth what I left behind

The INS man examines my knowledge of history
mouths my answers to his own questions:
E-man-ci-pation pro-cla-mation

Having to learn everything from scratch, reluctantly
unlearning a thousand things too, till what is left?

I come to America, one among millions
In this country of strangers
I make my way

SAFE

I lift my eyes to rain-stippled window panes.
In the sulphur sky the setting sun produces
not one, two rainbows—proof that the heavens
smile on our neighborhood. Across the alley
the houses beam like bright faces. Crows
cross the silver gilt clouds on smooth wings,
brush over copper maples and one black pine,
our dark protector. We are circled by arcs of promise,
held like chicks in a basket, assured that somehow
we will travel through winter, endure stark nights
and bare days, emerge in light. As if to affirm
the hope, the lower arc glows deep and glad,
glows and dissolves. The houses conceal
their joy. Alley lights come on like signals
to anxious watchers: Be easy. All is well.

The Gates of Life

My girls were never babies
they've always been women

my mother is making small talk
the dressmaker, mouth full of pins

kneels in front of me hemming
my mother's old Sunday skirt

they're turning it inside out for me
She's certainly tall for her age

her breasts are starting to bud
it won't be long now…

it won't be long now and what?
Stop fidgeting there's a dear

last night in a dream I saw
me in my blue school dress

so short that my knees stuck out
and I tried to pull down the sleeves to cover my wrists

I hid my hands in my pockets
so no one could see the inkstains

I was getting married and heard her say
Soon the gates of life will open for you

PROMISE

The judge, drunk, florid-faced,
speaks like someone balancing
on a high beam: *love, honor,*
obey, and we young fools
with difficulty suppress laughter,
say *yes, yes, till death do us part,*
can hardly wait to get outside
on the slushy Chicago street, back
to morning sickness, veterans' housing,
classes in medieval lit, with no thought
of all the years ahead, just walking
hand in hand as if a promise
had less weight than snowflakes
on a warm cheek.

CHILD LITTLE BODY

Child little body among other bodies
lying in the ship's dark belly in the
throb of engines coal dust everywhere
knees stiff arms hugging your chest
They said you take up too much space
Your mother is here somewhere
She cannot protect you
Your sisters cannot hug you The ship's
hollow shape keeps moving
through the night You do not matter now

There is hope You are
one of the lucky ones All this will
pass There will be no airplanes
this night You will wake with the
others and in the cool morning light
watch your mother cut bread and spread it
with honey Its sweetness will not
comfort you The bread will stick
in your throat But there will soon be
land again under your feet

No one has told you yet but there is still
kindness Drink it from this tin cup
There is help a blanket on a bed
in a ruined city You will learn again
honey is honey not the sweet bitterness
of longing for home Bread is bread
not the pain of separation A floor
is there to hold you up Your muscles
can unclench There is room enough And one day
a ship will be just a ship carrying ordinary people
to their ordinary destination

FROM THE EMPTY RAILROAD PLATFORM

we walked up the hill, Castle Street that was,
and looked for the address. There was no house,
no backyard, pump, no garden gate,
and where the beds had been, with tidy rows
of cabbages and beets, a thicket of tall trees
hid the view of a lake, below, that was no longer there.
Later, the town historian denied there'd ever been
a building there, as if we had invented our childhood.

[Title from a poem by Paul Zweig]

BOAT ON THE HIGH SEAS

On seeing Emil Nolde's watercolor

At first there is only the matte-black
mounded water grabbing out at you.

A treacherous eye of foam glints
pale green. You dread the wall

of darkness ahead. After the surge
sweeps you down with it

into the next glaucous hollow
there is a lull. Not long,

enough to see space, and a swath, beryl-
blue, flecked with white

brighter than the swirls of ashy clouds
on the horizon. Given time to breathe

you take in the turbulence above, its terrible
beauty, the depths above mirroring

peaks below. The sails you carry,
slashes of primrose yellow like the small

flowers picked in a season still emerging
from winter, lean into the waves.

They decide for you: that it is your greatest
desire to rise, be rocked, sustained

by this ascending,
plunging, living sea.

BALTIC IMPORTS

Easy and peaceful on the eyes, mittens hang tier upon tier: nut brown and pale wheat yellow, delicate green like unripe berries, tan like withered grasses, soot black, creamy white, the gray of winter clouds. "My aunties in Latvia knit them for me," explains the owner, she too in quiet colors like her wares. "The reds and blues get sold out first. I've told my knitters time and time again, Americans love their mittens bright and full of color. But do you think they listen? They're stubborn. They dye their yarn themselves with roots and flowers and leaves and bark. Those shades of color are way too subtle for our modern taste." I look down at my own scarf, fire engine red, my parka, electric blue. I would stick out like a sore thumb in the muted landscape of winter birches, gray woodsheds and saunas, dark plowed fields, a distant skyline of midnight blue firs. If I could have this morning's wish, I'd ask to blend into just such a landscape, wearing a coat of homespun gray, and quiet patterned mittens on my hands.

MELNEZERS—BLACK LAKE

They say the black firs
that made the water black and cold
are gone, and so perhaps
the lake is bog or marsh now, or
shrunk to a tepid pond.
I'll always know it deep and cold and black
and, cleaving the water, sleeker than a muskrat
with waterlilies in her mouth
there swims my mother. The flowers
are heavy and fragile. Drops
roll from the white petals. The smell is
on the edge between
sweetness and decomposing
soft reek of reeds and cattails.
My mother's white eyes and white teeth
laugh in her nut-brown face.
The lilies are for us.
She taught me how to make a necklace
the weighty flower head a pendant on my breast
the stalk delicate chains around my childish neck.
On the path home watching out
for gnarled roots and stones
we must have held her hands sometimes
and often must have lagged behind, called, *Wait!*
as shadows grew longer across the fields.
I don't remember that, only the peace
that still is conjured up by the familiar words:
ezers, lake, *ūdensrozes*, waterlilies.

ONLY WHEN WE SING

We were three sisters,
we all lived lovingly.
We wore one headdress,
shared one shawl.

Latvian folk song

Wasn't there enough
bread and jam
to go around?
Enough room
on our mother's lap
for us all?
No one was favored.

　　　　And yet my jealousy
　　　　spilled out like lava.
　　　　Devils and angels
　　　　in one breast.
　　　　It didn't take much
　　　　for rage to clench
　　　　my fists, hurl my body
　　　　upon my own sisters.

Little children,
love one another!
My mother's lament
burned itself
like phosphorus
into my brain.

　　　　All the sweeter
　　　　the brief loving
　　　　interludes:
　　　　drying the dishes
　　　　in the dim kitchen,

joining our voices
in song. Braiding
the little one's hair.
Playing with paper
dolls, putting them
gently to sleep
in their paper beds.

Wishing
that you'd fight back
give as hard
as you got
instead of sucking
your breath in
staring at me
dry-eyed.

All the time
walking the paper-thin
skin of earth
over the faultline.
Knowing
control was
just a matter of luck.
Not knowing when
the next eruption would be.

Hearing the song
in my head
about those three sisters
nestled like peas in a pod
under one shawl.

My Mother Said

When you drop
a piece of bread,
you have to
pick it up and
kiss it to show
you're sorry
for being careless
with this
precious gift of God.
Mother said *maizite*,
the tender, loving
diminutive
for *maize*, bread.
I bent down to retrieve it
kissed it reverently
to put things
right again
between us,
the bread and me.
Anyway, bread was never
it. Bread was
she, like mother,
like sun, like sea,
like earth,
and it was years
before I learned the difference
in foreign languages
between the animate
and the inanimate.

I Resemble No One

unless I listen
to my sister's
voice singing

my mother saying
dismissively
Oh, go on with you

unless I catch
that tired, haunted look
unexpectedly in a mirror

INVISIBILITY POEM: LESBIAN

There's quite enough to
identify her
should you have forgotten
her name:
That woman who lives in
who teaches
who speaks
who looks like
who writes about
the one who knows
the one who made
the one who loves to
who likes to wear
whose daughter
who used to be
wasn't she married to
didn't she once spend some time
Every known thing about her
is like a smell
reassuring, familiar
"She is like   us"
"We are like   her"
No need to watch suspiciously
when she walks by.
Not as familiar perhaps
the things she keeps
invisible:
the woman with whom
the circle of friends that she
the way she feels when
the thoughts she doesn't
the fear that keeps her from
the times she imagines
the price she pays for

ALWAYS DIFFERENT, ALWAYS THE SAME

Based on a line by Paul Zweig

Always different, always the same
the sky, which we both watch,
in different cities, far apart.
A grey day, I say. *Glorious sunshine*,
you reply. Other times, we search
for words to describe colors, movement,
cloud shapes, how they evolve,
because *wonderful* does not seem enough.

A HEART

A heart that thinks it's a prisoner
in a cage, when really it is a dog
barking, barking behind a white fence
bewildered by change, any change:
these strangers passing by
whom it does not recognize
even when they reach out a hand
even when they call it by name

WE

Listen to the way people in couples
unlearn to say *I*: *We*, they say, *us* and *our*.
Oh, haven't I also tried to lose
my *I* in a safe *we*? Father and mother,
sisters; the kids; and all those twosomes
with this lover and that. We eating
soup and bread, we in the woods
side by side uphill and down, we tired
after a day harvesting, we lying in bed
reading. Perhaps a tribal urge: after
dark around a fire together, warm;
or memories of a rural past—mowing
a field, moving in rhythm, scythes flashing,
or in the house spinning, knitting
as the tallow candle burns lower, sputters out,
then hearing the sleepers' breaths
from every corner of the room. —
But then, there's always been the thoughtful,
the glad, the solitary *I*: under
the apple tree crying, or crossing
a meadow, shoes *full of blue petals*,
golden dew, or singing on a hilltop.
Going away to be filled, tasting, knowing,
with eyes open, even in fear, even
in pain. Then bringing her riches to the *we*.

CRESCENT MOON

Yesterday, the wind rose.
The air had been so mild,
the streets holiday quiet,
all those yellow leaves
under the maples near my house.
They meant to lie there forever.
The wind rose and disorder
arrived, and chill, and frightening
sights: a sickle moon too shiny,
in league with Venus preternaturally
bright. In the park, mounds of leaf
mold where roses had bloomed.
Shoals of black silhouettes in the lake,
waterbirds waiting until it's time
to go. Early jets inching up, lights blinking,
leaving, leaving. I thought of you
telling me: We can't go on like this.

ESSENCE

The satisfaction of cleaning up after a party:
damp napkins in the trampled grass,
cigarette butts, a child's barrette, glasses with half-
moons of burgundy lees, the laths that held up
a wet marquee piled tidily on sawhorses in the barn.
The rain continues steadily, soaks the black
earth. We work without speaking (only an infrequent
nod), restoring silence, order, emptiness even,
as though the gathering of friends
must be made invisible, abstract, mere memory,
every trace removed; as though this is life
in its essence—lights extinguished, chairs stacked
along the basement wall, every crumb
of the feast swept up, taken out with the trash.

ENDING

It was easier than it sounds.
Nothing dramatic, nothing sudden,
no point where either of them could have said:
Something has come between us.
They moved one past the other
like figures in a weatherhouse:
when one went in, the other must
emerge. The little cottage
did not have room enough for two.
She thought that every winter
is followed by a spring, she watched
for thaw, for buds to break
open, for the arrival of singing
birds, and the first scouts from beehives.
Their life had seemed a fact
predictable as suns rising
and setting and rising forever.
Like her ancestors in distant times
she made offerings and prayed
to bring the sun back
and thought it would return if only
she knew the right words. It took time
for her to learn new phrases
to describe what had happened:
over, not any more, there was
nothing we could have done.

ABSENCE

Variegated skies with silhouettes of winter
trees. That dreamy dip in the road, the drive
across the bridge, the quiet river
almost subdued by ice—
even without you I've been happy,
but this is too much:
early morning, new snow, clean and soft,
marked only by the delicate feet of birds,
everything, everything asking to be loved,
even the plum tree's branch that rubs
my shoulder as I wade past
to the garage.
                    Let me
be miserable for a while,
let me close up like a fist, and hug
your absence to my numb
heart. Later, I don't know when,
I'll let myself be happy,
and by then passing feet
will have made paths, trucks will roar by
scattering salt and sand,
and planes will be crossing
distances.

WHAT IS INEVITABLE

Nous n'irons plus au bois
Folk song

We know of course
what is inevitable
in this life.

We will no longer
pick golden mushrooms
under pines

or sleep spoonfashion
breast against a lover's
damp warm back

or watch a green
tornado sky
feeling sure

we'll be unscathed.
We'll lick our pencils:
simple math

and the equation's
other side will get
shorter. How

learn compassion?
How teach our eyes
not to look

away when death
rolls by on the street
on four wheels?

How love with joy
when the conductor blows
his whistle? How

unlearn desire?
Knowing the answer, we don't want
to know it.

Closeted Lesbian Infiltrates Latvian Knitters' Group

All the women are frankly curious,
their eyes light up at my *labdien*.
Cast on two hundred twenty stitches.

A new face. *Miller? Miller? You wouldn't*
be Doctor Miller's daughter? Oh, you're not?
Increase one stitch at end of next two rows.

It's not your maiden name? You've lived
here how long? Twenty years already?
Put half the stitches on a holder, knit the rest.

Don't think I've ever seen you at the Latvian House.
Which congregation would you be in?
Knit two together, make one, two together.

I'm the black sheep. I married wrong.
I didn't send my kids to Latvian school.
Repeat the pattern eight more times.

I didn't come to church. I never joined
the Latvian choir or went to song fests.
Cast off ten center stitches.

It's bad enough that I'm a vegetarian.
There's more to come, for I'm a lesbian, too.
Decrease two stitches next ten rows.

If I were shy I'd turn into a mouse
and run away. But I'm enjoying this.
Knit two, purl two, repeat till end of row.

How nice to be the focus of attention—
excitement surges round the room.
Increase ten stitches spacing evenly.

And sitting here among my grizzled
contemporaries, how young I feel!
Purl twelve, turn work, knit twelve.

We could have all been schoolmates, wives
and mothers, going through life together.
Work even from the chart until the end.

You followed old recipes, made Latvian
cheese, baked yellow saffron bread.
Work thirty stitches, place on holder.

I went to demonstrations, walked
in Gay Pride marches, tried to be p.c.
Follow Chart B, work back and forth.

What difference does it make? The needles
click, we sit companionably together.
Work knit rows right to left and purl rows left to right.

Without great urgency our talk unrolls
like yarn, familiar words in our familiar tongue.
Break yarn, pass through last stitch. Repeat for other side.

The House on Hen's Feet

It wasn't the tasks along the way,
the cow with the swollen udder
who needed milking, the panting ewe
who asked to be shorn, the apple tree
laden with ripe fruit I had to pick,
or the brown loaves that cried to me
from the oven. It wasn't fear of the ogre
retreating sly-eyed to sharpen his knife
in his house on hen's feet. It was
the homecoming, when I knew
she had meant to send me to my death,
and the sudden attention they paid me,
me and the ogre's gold.

GYROMITRA MERULIOIDES

velvet brown ears in the grass
by the ash tree, open
to every question:
                          Am I my sister's
keeper? Where does my responsibility
end? And if she mistrusts me?
tells me, *Don't loom over me?*

How deep does forgiveness
need to go? Is it forgiveness
if lurking under the surface
blame lies like bile, almost biblical in intensity,
waiting to spew forth?

Can I wish good to one
who hurt me? Can I love?

To you other living things
these human questions
are no questions at all.
Touched by a hard hand
you gyromitras turn color
but do not retaliate.

Neither do you ask questions,
or torture yourselves
in the early hours as the city
begins to wake.

Soon you'll be gone,
and I still have no answers,
tender listeners,
little velvet brown ears.

POSTCARDS

The painters are coming tomorrow. I take down Anaïs Nin, Colette, Cindy Sherman as catwoman, three black-robed nuns at the beach dancing in the waves, women on a park bench, their stockings rolled down. Gone the family around the stove in their house in Costa Rica, the father with his guitar, the mom at the ironing board, the two little sisters, heads bent toward each other, in a room that is turquoise and mauve, bloodred and pink. Gone the cantaloupe, split, showing a hundred seeds; the night sky washed with northern lights; the tree in whose branches perches a pale bird of a crescent moon. Like a capricious deity I choose which ones will survive: tulips, moccasin flowers, hepaticas, the Dolomiti in morning mist, a cottage in Ireland and cows coming home on a road bordered with green, green grass. I shouldn't have read the messages on the back, greetings from the dead, the vanished, with reassurances we'll see each other soon, and sending much love.

People hardly write postcards anymore. In a remote town in the middle of Swabia or Michoacán, you can walk into a cybercafé, order Orangina, send off an e-mail evanescent as streaks of cloud. Far away, a friend reads it, presses *delete.* So you buy postcards: Frida Kahlo with parrots on her shoulders, alpine flowers, Diego's round face, ancient aqueducts. You hope for solidity. As though no one could shred the evidence that there's a bond between all of us.

WHAT I WILL MOST LONG FOR

When I'm dead
there'll be all that time before
the body becomes moist crumbly soil

I know I'll long for the feeling
of hair bouncing, just washed
fragrant, and me invulnerable
staring down cars at intersections
a coat flung over my shoulders

What am I saying, I long for it now
and tenderness, that melting to touch
turned liquid, reckless, and without fear

7:30 A.M. BLUES

Woke up this morning
Tried to tune out the news

Woke up this morning
My dreams were full of the news

My dreams were eerie
Radiation's changing us all

My dreams were so eerie
Radiation everywhere

She said she liked me
I had a big smile on my face

She said she liked me
I had a great big smile on my face

I drove in the traffic
Listening to the blues

Zero degrees and holding
I was laughing out loud

Zero degrees and still holding
Got to stay safe and warm

Sending out my own signal:
World, I'm still your fan

Sending out a clear signal:
World, I am your fan

PRESENCES

There are presences in the old cedars
so loud with joy only airplanes can drown
them out—who move on twittering wings
so quick they barely register on retinas,

and yesterday the holy ghost
like a gray pigeon quietly slipped
past the broken slats under the neighbor's
eaves. Then who am I to mutter,

He ought to call the pest control?
or to reply, *Same old, same old*
when they ask me, *Hey, how's life?*
We're hanging out the weekly wash

and in a wavering hook over our heads
trumpeters sweep the evening sky
sounding their way north like high trombones
without a lower register.

Raking his lawn on Thirteenth Avenue
the young man with the black wool cap
looked at me with the melting eyes
of a believer. "Yes, I saw them,

Jesus, Buddha, and the angels flying
over."—"Swans," I said.—"Swan princes,"
he said, "all the swan princes in the world
chanting en route to paradise."

JUNE

You know there will be a surprise
and yet it is always a surprise
the taste of wild strawberries on the tip
of the tongue, friendly yet sour
just slightly rough and dry like the slope
they grew on; and somewhere as it lingers
in the mouth there's a shock of sweetness
the intoxication of fragrance inside your head
psychedelic rush of noonday heat, silence
interrupted by whispering insects, blood and
its din in the temples, the banging of
the heart against your chest. You are
eating summer, it melts and slides
down your throat, yet without sadness.
You know that this will come again
and again, and perhaps death too will come
like a small compact red surprise.

INFANT ICU

Your skin is
thin, like fillo dough, more fragile than
old muslin in an antique shop,
but your rosy body underneath
is so alive that every vein is visible
pulsing with blood, and your limbs
respond to signals only you can sense
as though a puppeteer had pulled
on sudden strings.
Oh baby, there you lie under the white
light exposed, naked before our gaze
open as I hope you never need to be
without consent again.
But, since you know no shame,
undistracted, like a thinker deep in thought
you focus on each need
and behind eyelids clenched to keep sight out
home in on what your body asks
and cry it out aloud with that
shocking trust that there will be
ears to hear and hands to help,
warmth to envelop
you, so unprepared a visitor
to this cold planet
so insufficiently briefed.

In Treatment

My friend lies in his narrow trundle bed.
Pain comes in waves where radiation
zapped his throat and mouth. Now I hear
his footsteps creak downstairs. He flicks
the kitchen switch, his eyes close in a squint
against the glare. He fills a glass. The water
cuts his muscles like shards of ice.

The dark: Dogs signal to each other
through cyclone fences. Somewhere
in the city thin snakes of sound curl
into distance, police car sirens nervous
as a drugged body. A faucet keeps
slow time. Below the window
in the garden magnolia petals

glow pale like lights someone forgot
to put out. My friend sits at the table,
writes postcards to his students:
*Hola! All rumors to the contrary
I will not return this spring.* He signs
jauntily, licks blue jay stamps,
returns to bed. Morphine thoughts

echo through his head. Sleep teases,
comes closer, retreats again. At last
lets itself be petted, held close. Through shallow
dreams, the sparrows' first drowsy cheeps
greet a gray dawn. The morning paper.
A crossword puzzle. I know he'll read me
my horoscope: a promise of happiness.

ONIONS

We're playing
for high stakes—

You advance your planes
carrying destruction:
Here are two hawks, wings outspread
above tawny trees

Your helicopters disrupt the silence
churn up the ground:
Here's the last bumblebee on late
gold chrysanthemums

You have uniformed soldiers, young faces
tired in the morning light:
I've only crows calling to each other
over the slough

You challenge me with thousands
of pounds of bombs
I have these seven onions so big my hands
can barely cup them

Let's see who wins—
your bombs, my onions

AUTUMN MORNING

Trying to stay
in love with the world—
the rehearsal room floor
all those beautiful strips of wood
each different, crazy grain, whorls, streaks;
the neighbors' little dog
whimpering in the cold dawn.
If I go through the motions,
will I be whole again?
Three small dark birds on the power line
make a pattern without meaning.
The icebox starts to hum.
Planes fly overhead. At breakfast
my mother always looks out
to see if the wind is in the elms.
I tell her, "There is no wind.
The leaves are changing color.
It's going to be another fine day."

BEACH. BLACKBOARD

for my mother

The beach doesn't know
all the inscriptions
lovers and children left on it
are gone, washed away
by the rising tide.
And the night's flotsam
will be gone by morning.
The beach doesn't long
to have it back.

The board doesn't mutter
in confusion because a hand
dragged a wet sponge
methodically up and down,
up and down, so that now
all the names have vanished,
the formulae, the facts.
The board is squeaky clean
for the next lesson.

Oh that a mind could hold
still at such loss.

LONG ENOUGH

All right, I say, all right,
it's been long enough,
time for you to come back,
undo the work of the flames,
undo the leaden-limbed silence
on the mortuary table,
the bloodspattered arrival
in the wailing ambulance,
time to be at the intersection
with the kneeling woman
who held your hands,
reassuring, "You're going
to be all right, they'll take good
care of you," and then time
to stand on the corner waiting
for the light to turn green,
and when the truck careens
onto the sidewalk, to step back
gracefully so that the blow misses
you and your sturdy bike,
so you can resume the ride
to the south side of town
where we need you, where
we have taken back our grief,
and winter will resume
like a film rewound to the part
where the sound broke off,
while the audience turns to the screen again
as though nothing had happened.

DEATH

Travel to strange countries
is not so frightening
when I know I'll be met
at the airport, or someone
will be waiting when the bus
pulls up at a crossroads:
Mexico, Denmark, Russia...

And now *you* are in Death,
permanently, a resident's visa.
I've changed my mind about never
wanting to go, you are the best reason
for making travel plans.

MOTH

Not the kind housewives
try to slap midair,
small, elusive, grey.
No, a great big slow one,

an odalisque who lets you
gaze at her beauty,
turns her head a little:
Look your fill.

APPLES

Another crazy generous
gesture the universe lavishes
on us—except it doesn't even
have us in mind, it doesn't
care: above—dragging the branches
earthward, below—cradled
in wet grass, take them
or leave them. And, *Thank you,*
I say, *thank you*
ever so much!

HOMECOMING

I thought my heart might burst:
I slowed it down, I kept it still.
I hadn't counted on the red-rimmed eye
of a narcissus blinking up at me,
or the pale primroses' sweet scent
piercing the shield of years
and striking home unerringly.
I didn't cry, but for a while
each detail of the landscape we drove through
swam before my eyes larger than memories.

*

A place where I felt known.
Everybody
said my name
right.

*

Since my return
my heart side goes numb at night.
The salt of unwept tears
stings my throat.

*

I had a wonderful time.
I had a terrible time.
I wished I could stay forever.
I counted the days,
impatient to get back here.

*

When I was there, I spoke of home,
this house in Minneapolis.
Now I catch myself saying,
I went home last summer.

*

If this house is home,
there are certain
implications. I must plant
apple trees, plums, and a cherry.
But what I need most are
at least three black currant bushes,
my backyard
just like my cousin's yard
at the edge of the woods
on the outskirts of Riga.

GETTING TO KNOW YOUR OWN CHARACTER

Pots and pans
Do you wash them to impress your roommate?
Has it ever occurred to you that the rings
of rust in the sink might make a fine pattern?

Boxes
How many presents will you have to buy
to fill all those boxes
you've saved on the basement shelves?

Daydreaming
Can you let the thoughts go soaring over the cottonwood
without calling them back to perch on your shoulder?

Beetles that come from nowhere
Is it important to know that big black beetle's
Latin name? Isn't it enough to admire
the bluish sheen of its wings?

Noises in the dark
Who did you think it was?
Did a shade of guilt pass over your heart?

When time seems to stop
In the morning kitchen once more. Must you
eat granola every day of the year?

The mail arrives
What exactly is it you long for?

Heat
What will it take to get warm?

After a hard night
Next time, will you please remember it all
shrinks back to size by morning, and the bit
just before the alarm clock rings is especially sweet?

In outer space
From up there in outer space, will you wave
to the tiny house, the maple trees and the lilacs
while you are still able to see them, and before
they are swallowed by the smudge of cloud
on the face of the blue-green planet?

LAIMA, GODDESS OF FATE

When I opened my mouth
for my first wail
she was there. She showed me
the gifts she had for me:
a cobblestone road
a goose feather quill
a dandelion seed
a russet apple
a pair of sturdy shoes.
I grew into the shoes
to walk the cobblestone road
to the world
and learned to write my name
with the goose feather quill.
The dandelion seed
linked me
to earth and sun.
The apple taught my mouth
the sour and the sweet
taste of life.
And don't forget
to sing sometimes,
said fate.

INSTRUCTIONS

Such a hard assignment: *Say what you love.*
Name a benign creature
you are not afraid of.

The answer emerges terrible:
Too often this heart merely
goes through the motions.

Loving is a road to loss. Even a child's
little hand can wield destruction—
roots pulled up, flowers crushed.

And all the other endings—separation,
indifference. No need to mention
gods or governments.

So here are my instructions: Eyes,
do not dry up. Lungs, breathe deep,
give strength to shouts and songs.

And you, my heart, you have a lifelong task
to be a gate. Closing. Opening.
No matter what, no matter who

demands to be let in. You are only
the gate. No judgment, no questions,
no fear, my heart, but courage.

Rediscovering an Ancient Word

in Fowles's *The French Lieutenant's Woman*

I roll it around in my mouth like a kid given one of those hard red candies who smiles, looks down at her bare toes. *Haulm*. A country word that goes back a long way into a time when people still sat around on hot days under the biggest tree in the village square, or in the shadow of a hedge, white shirts blue in the light that reaches through leaves. Haulm. The knots at the points where the sections connect make it strong as the hands of a farmer after a lifetime of work. Paradox: how it bends in the wind, gives, obeys, sways, has something to teach—toughness, humility, when it stands up after a storm or, bent to the ground, kisses its own death.

Why This Question Has No Answer

How are you? they ask—
a difficult question
though spring is back
and everything is easy
even paying a parking ticket
incurred when you stopped the car
and before you knew it
had walked halfway around a lake
bordered by saskatoon almost in flower
and willows for whose green you need a new word.

You pick plum blossoms
to take to a party celebrating
a brand-new triangular house on a corner lot
built to be filled with loud music
and the running footsteps of the owner's many nieces.
You wake up in the morning and your body feels good.
Every joint is oiled.
You're hungry for wild greens
scrambled eggs and corn bread.

And still when they ask that question
you hesitate. It is war.
You try to send your body's ease
and the joy of your senses
to the suffering ones. You try to breathe
the smoke of their pain as you were taught.
You don't know how to answer.

LIVE OUT THE YEARS

In the hands of God now and always
the dead, simplified to bones, and life
teeming with blessings on this kind day.

Trees coursing with sap. Shivering pale
against the neighbor's white wall
what were garlands of roses, and will be again.

Butterflies waiting to emerge, to sip from the mud.
All this water, greening the grass, raising
yellow lilies to shine their light on the world.

The sun pouring her love on my small orchard,
Saint Mary's cemetery spread out over the hill, a cyclone
fence holding plastic scraps sent by the wind,

the loud brook, dandelion flowers puddling golden
around even the bleakest buildings
where humans live out their years.

THE POEM OF MY LIFE

I want to show her one poem which is the poem of my life
Adrienne Rich

I must write it new, for all my work lies behind me like the dry skin of a snake.

Can a sheet of paper hold it? Yes, if it stretches from horizon to horizon, but barely.

Will there be room for all the trees that come crowding into the poem's space, and the smooth damp paths my feet have walked on over the years?

Can the poem contain the springs from which I have scooped water in my cupped hands, or the faintly bitter cress that grew near them in the shade?

I don't want to leave out a single fruit I have bitten into with my sharp teeth. I want the poem to taste like early green apples, like the first wild strawberries in June, like the sweetest pineapple, perfuming the air, so delicious it must be eaten with eyes closed.

Have I put in all the other tastes: the thin acidity of wood sorrel flowers, the utmost fire of even the smallest pili pili pepper, the good sting of garlic, the pain of honey, the calmness of clabbered milk?

And the flowers, each in its season, calling out to humans and moths and hummingbirds with their fragrance and glowing color, swelling to seed, taking on endings as gladly as they do beginnings.

How do I record the arrivals and departures that have taught my arms to close in an embrace or open and let go?

And the days I spent waiting for something that never came, or lying restlessly in the grass looking up at the clouds.

This poem knows embarrassment and joy and grief and fury and bliss and shame. In it are traces of times when I wished I could die and times when I wished a moment would last forever.

The poem has heard the crying of babies, the howls of bomb alarms, the moans of a lover's ecstasies, the morning declarations of crows, hum of slow distant traffic, crickets endlessly shrilling on hot August nights.

I can't leave out the vastness of caves in fever nightmares, the comfort of curling up in the shelter of sheets and blankets, or the distances during orgasm that rush further and further into blinding infinity.

Roads unfurling under the tires of an old car, wind in one's hair as one runs a race to the end of the field, the small terror of feeling the downhill momentum when limbs seem to move without volition toward a fall.

I haven't even begun to put in the faces, the bodies, the arms legs mouths hands I have touched, that have touched me.

And light shimmering, glinting, beaming, refracted into a thousand colors, or swallowed by the dark, diffused by clouds or dust or mental anguish.

This cannot be the poem to honor sufficiently the many miracles I have seen: all that was created by ineffable forces, or even all the things made by human hands and tools and instruments, each more delightful than the last.

I have not even spoken of all the connections between the beings that inhabit our world—Mozart sonatas, Brueghel, bridges, tall shining buildings, singing together, the poems that enter our hearts and remain there becoming a part of us. Forgive me for leaving out so much.

ILZE KĻAVIŅA MUELLER, a Minnesotan for thirty years, emigrated from Latvia during World War II. Her poetry reflects her range of languages and cultures and her interest in travel. She divides her time between translation and poetry. Her poems have appeared in *Looking for Home: Women Writing about Exile, CALYX, Water~Stone, 100 Words, Hedgebrook Journal,* and *Deeper Than You Think,* and her translations include Christa Reinig's *Idleness Is the Root of All Love* and texts in *The Review of Contemporary Fiction* (Spring 1998) and *Leading Contemporary Poets* (Western Michigan University).

L A U R E L
P O E T R Y
COLLECTIVE

A gathering of twenty-three poets and graphic artists living in the Twin Cities area, the Laurel Poetry Collective is a self-funded collaboration dedicated to publishing beautiful and affordable books, chapbooks, and broadsides. Started in 2002, its four-year charter is to publish and celebrate, one by one, a book or chapbook by each of its twenty-one poet members. The Laurel members are: Lisa Ann Berg, Teresa Boyer, Annie Breitenbucher, Margot Fortunato Galt, Georgia A. Greeley, Ann Sarah Iverson, Mary L. Junge, Deborah Keenan, Joyce Kennedy, Ilze Kļaviņa Mueller, Yvette Nelson, Eileen O'Toole, Kathy Alma Peterson, Regula Russelle, Sylvia Ruud, Tom Ruud, Su Smallen, Susanna Styve, Suzanne Swanson, Nancy M. Walden, Lois Welshons, Pam Wynn, Nolan Zavoral.

For current information about the series—including broad-sides, subscriptions, and single copy purchase—visit:

www.laurelpoetry.com

or write:

Laurel Poetry Collective
1168 Laurel Avenue
St. Paul, MN 55104